50 Canadian Breakfast Dishes for Home

By: Kelly Johnson

Table of Contents

- Classic Canadian Pancakes
- Maple Syrup French Toast
- Peameal Bacon and Eggs
- Buttermilk Blueberry Pancakes
- Montreal-Style Bagels with Cream Cheese
- Nanaimo Bar Oatmeal
- Prairie Wheat Porridge
- Wild Blueberry Muffins
- Maple-Glazed Bacon
- Saskatoon Berry Scones
- Baked Oatmeal with Maple Syrup
- Tourtière Breakfast Hand Pies
- Cheddar and Chive Biscuits with Sausage Gravy
- Honey Butter Bannock
- Apple and Cinnamon Oatmeal
- Farmer's Market Veggie Omelet
- Roasted Root Vegetable Hash
- Smoked Salmon and Cream Cheese Bagel
- Cranberry Maple Granola
- Wild Rice and Mushroom Frittata
- Chokecherry Syrup Pancakes
- Cornmeal Johnny Cakes with Maple Butter
- Rye Toast with Homemade Berry Jam
- Maple Pecan Sticky Buns
- Bison Sausage and Egg Breakfast Sandwich
- Apple Butter Toast with Canadian Cheddar
- Classic Poutine Breakfast Bowl
- Maple Glazed Donuts
- Grilled Arctic Char and Poached Egg Toast
- Cranberry Walnut Breakfast Bread
- Maple Walnut Granola Bars
- Smoked Trout and Dill Scramble
- French Canadian Crêpes
- Bacon and Egg Bannock Sandwich
- Maple Baked Beans on Toast

- Roasted Pumpkin and Spice Muffins
- Wild Berry Yogurt Parfait
- Cheddar and Apple Omelet
- Saskatoon Berry Breakfast Crisp
- Sweet Corn Fritters with Honey Butter
- Maple Cinnamon Overnight Oats
- Classic Western Sandwich
- Butter Tart Waffles
- Roasted Hazelnut and Maple Porridge
- Cranberry and Sunflower Seed Energy Bites
- Canadian Bacon Breakfast Pizza
- Caramelized Apple Pancakes
- Peameal Bacon Eggs Benedict
- Maple Chia Seed Pudding
- Homemade Rhubarb Jam on Toast

Classic Canadian Pancakes

Ingredients:

- 1 1/2 cups all-purpose flour
- 1 tbsp sugar
- 1 tbsp baking powder
- 1/2 tsp salt
- 1 1/4 cups milk
- 1 egg
- 2 tbsp melted butter
- 1 tsp vanilla extract

Instructions:

1. In a bowl, whisk together flour, sugar, baking powder, and salt.
2. In another bowl, mix milk, egg, melted butter, and vanilla.
3. Combine wet and dry ingredients, stirring until just mixed.
4. Heat a skillet over medium heat and grease lightly.
5. Pour batter onto skillet and cook until bubbles form, then flip and cook until golden brown.
6. Serve warm with maple syrup.

Maple Syrup French Toast

Ingredients:

- 4 slices thick bread
- 2 eggs
- 1/2 cup milk
- 1 tsp vanilla extract
- 1/2 tsp cinnamon
- 2 tbsp butter
- Maple syrup for serving

Instructions:

1. In a bowl, whisk eggs, milk, vanilla, and cinnamon.
2. Dip bread slices into mixture, coating both sides.
3. Heat butter in a skillet and cook bread until golden brown on each side.
4. Serve with warm maple syrup.

Peameal Bacon and Eggs

Ingredients:

- 6 slices peameal bacon
- 2 eggs
- 1 tbsp butter
- Salt and pepper to taste

Instructions:

1. Heat a skillet over medium heat and cook peameal bacon for 2-3 minutes per side until golden.
2. In a separate pan, melt butter and fry eggs to desired doneness.
3. Season eggs with salt and pepper and serve with bacon.

Buttermilk Blueberry Pancakes

Ingredients:

- 1 1/2 cups all-purpose flour
- 1 tbsp sugar
- 1 tsp baking soda
- 1/2 tsp salt
- 1 1/4 cups buttermilk
- 1 egg
- 2 tbsp melted butter
- 1 cup fresh or frozen blueberries

Instructions:

1. In a bowl, mix flour, sugar, baking soda, and salt.
2. In another bowl, whisk buttermilk, egg, and melted butter.
3. Combine wet and dry ingredients, then fold in blueberries.
4. Cook pancakes on a greased skillet over medium heat until bubbles form, then flip and cook until golden.
5. Serve warm with maple syrup.

Montreal-Style Bagels with Cream Cheese

Ingredients:

- 2 Montreal-style bagels
- 1/2 cup cream cheese
- 1 tbsp honey
- 1 tbsp chopped chives (optional)

Instructions:

1. Slice bagels in half and toast until golden.
2. Spread cream cheese evenly on each half.
3. Drizzle with honey and sprinkle with chives if desired.

Nanaimo Bar Oatmeal

Ingredients:

- 1 cup rolled oats
- 2 cups milk or water
- 1 tbsp cocoa powder
- 1 tbsp maple syrup
- 1/4 cup shredded coconut
- 1/4 cup chocolate chips
- 1 tbsp butter

Instructions:

1. In a saucepan, bring milk to a simmer and stir in oats, cocoa powder, and maple syrup.
2. Cook for 5 minutes, stirring occasionally.
3. Stir in shredded coconut and butter.
4. Top with chocolate chips before serving.

Prairie Wheat Porridge

Ingredients:

- 1/2 cup wheat berries
- 2 cups water
- 1/2 cup milk
- 1 tbsp maple syrup
- 1/2 tsp cinnamon

Instructions:

1. Rinse wheat berries and soak overnight.
2. Drain and simmer in water for 30-40 minutes until tender.
3. Stir in milk, maple syrup, and cinnamon. Serve warm.

Wild Blueberry Muffins

Ingredients:

- 2 cups all-purpose flour
- 1/2 cup sugar
- 1 tbsp baking powder
- 1/2 tsp salt
- 1 cup wild blueberries
- 1 cup milk
- 1/3 cup butter, melted
- 1 egg
- 1 tsp vanilla extract

Instructions:

1. Preheat oven to 375°F (190°C).
2. In a bowl, mix flour, sugar, baking powder, and salt.
3. In another bowl, whisk milk, butter, egg, and vanilla.
4. Combine wet and dry ingredients, then fold in blueberries.
5. Spoon batter into muffin tin and bake for 18-20 minutes.

Maple-Glazed Bacon

Ingredients:

- 6 slices bacon
- 2 tbsp maple syrup

Instructions:

1. Preheat oven to 375°F (190°C).
2. Lay bacon on a baking sheet and brush with maple syrup.
3. Bake for 12-15 minutes until crispy.

Saskatoon Berry Scones

Ingredients:

- 2 cups all-purpose flour
- 1/4 cup sugar
- 1 tbsp baking powder
- 1/2 tsp salt
- 1/2 cup cold butter, cubed
- 1/2 cup milk
- 1 egg
- 1 tsp vanilla extract
- 1 cup Saskatoon berries

Instructions:

1. Preheat oven to 375°F (190°C).
2. Mix flour, sugar, baking powder, and salt.
3. Cut in butter until mixture is crumbly.
4. Whisk milk, egg, and vanilla, then add to dry ingredients.
5. Fold in Saskatoon berries. Shape dough into a disc and cut into wedges.
6. Bake for 18-20 minutes until golden.

Baked Oatmeal with Maple Syrup

Ingredients:

- 2 cups rolled oats
- 1/4 cup maple syrup
- 1 tsp baking powder
- 1/2 tsp cinnamon
- 1/4 tsp salt
- 1 1/2 cups milk
- 1 egg
- 1 tsp vanilla extract
- 1 tbsp melted butter

Instructions:

1. Preheat oven to 350°F (175°C).
2. In a bowl, mix oats, baking powder, cinnamon, and salt.
3. In another bowl, whisk milk, egg, vanilla, maple syrup, and butter.
4. Combine with oat mixture and pour into a greased baking dish.
5. Bake for 30-35 minutes until golden brown. Serve warm.

Tourtière Breakfast Hand Pies

Ingredients:

Filling:

- 1/2 lb ground pork
- 1/2 small onion, finely chopped
- 1 clove garlic, minced
- 1/4 tsp ground cinnamon
- 1/4 tsp ground cloves
- 1/4 tsp dried thyme
- 1/4 tsp salt
- 1/8 tsp black pepper
- 1/4 cup mashed potatoes

Pastry:

- 2 cups all-purpose flour
- 1/2 tsp salt
- 1/2 cup cold butter, cubed
- 1/4 cup cold water
- 1 egg, beaten (for egg wash)

Instructions:

1. In a skillet, cook pork, onion, and garlic until browned. Stir in spices and mashed potatoes. Let cool.
2. Mix flour and salt, cut in butter, and add water until dough forms. Chill for 30 minutes.
3. Roll out dough and cut into circles. Fill with meat mixture, fold, and seal edges.
4. Brush with egg wash and bake at 375°F (190°C) for 20-25 minutes until golden brown.

Cheddar and Chive Biscuits with Sausage Gravy

Ingredients:

Biscuits:

- 2 cups all-purpose flour
- 1 tbsp baking powder
- 1/2 tsp salt
- 1/2 cup cold butter, cubed
- 1 cup shredded cheddar cheese
- 1/4 cup chopped chives
- 3/4 cup milk

Gravy:

- 1/2 lb breakfast sausage
- 2 tbsp butter
- 2 tbsp flour
- 2 cups milk
- 1/2 tsp black pepper
- Salt to taste

Instructions:

1. Mix biscuit dry ingredients, cut in butter, and stir in cheese and chives. Add milk and mix until dough forms.
2. Drop spoonfuls onto a baking sheet and bake at 375°F (190°C) for 15-18 minutes.
3. Cook sausage in a skillet, add butter and flour, stirring for 1 minute. Slowly whisk in milk.
4. Simmer until thickened, season with salt and pepper. Serve over biscuits.

Honey Butter Bannock

Ingredients:

- 2 cups all-purpose flour
- 1 tbsp baking powder
- 1/2 tsp salt
- 1/4 cup butter, melted
- 3/4 cup water
- 2 tbsp honey

Instructions:

1. Mix flour, baking powder, and salt in a bowl.
2. Stir in melted butter, water, and honey until dough forms.
3. Shape into a round and bake at 375°F (190°C) for 25-30 minutes.
4. Serve warm with extra honey butter.

Apple and Cinnamon Oatmeal

Ingredients:

- 1 cup rolled oats
- 2 cups milk or water
- 1 apple, diced
- 1 tbsp maple syrup
- 1/2 tsp cinnamon

Instructions:

1. Bring milk to a simmer, stir in oats and diced apple.
2. Cook for 5 minutes, stirring occasionally.
3. Stir in maple syrup and cinnamon. Serve warm.

Farmer's Market Veggie Omelet

Ingredients:

- 3 eggs
- 1 tbsp milk
- 1/4 cup bell peppers, diced
- 1/4 cup mushrooms, sliced
- 1/4 cup spinach
- 1 tbsp butter
- Salt and pepper to taste

Instructions:

1. Whisk eggs with milk, salt, and pepper.
2. Sauté vegetables in butter until tender.
3. Pour eggs over vegetables and cook until set. Fold and serve warm.

Roasted Root Vegetable Hash

Ingredients:

- 1 sweet potato, diced
- 1 Yukon gold potato, diced
- 1 carrot, diced
- 1 parsnip, diced
- 1 small onion, chopped
- 2 tbsp olive oil
- 1/2 tsp salt
- 1/4 tsp black pepper

Instructions:

1. Toss vegetables with olive oil, salt, and pepper.
2. Spread on a baking sheet and roast at 400°F (200°C) for 25-30 minutes, stirring occasionally.
3. Serve warm with eggs or sausage.

Smoked Salmon and Cream Cheese Bagel

Ingredients:

- 1 Montreal-style bagel, sliced
- 2 tbsp cream cheese
- 2 oz smoked salmon
- 1 tbsp capers
- 1 tbsp red onion, sliced
- 1 tsp lemon juice

Instructions:

1. Toast bagel halves.
2. Spread cream cheese on each half.
3. Top with smoked salmon, capers, red onion, and a squeeze of lemon juice.

Cranberry Maple Granola

Ingredients:

- 2 cups rolled oats
- 1/2 cup chopped pecans
- 1/4 cup sunflower seeds
- 1/4 cup dried cranberries
- 1/4 cup maple syrup
- 2 tbsp coconut oil
- 1/2 tsp cinnamon

Instructions:

1. Mix oats, pecans, and sunflower seeds in a bowl.
2. Heat maple syrup, coconut oil, and cinnamon, then pour over oat mixture. Toss to coat.
3. Spread on a baking sheet and bake at 325°F (165°C) for 20 minutes, stirring halfway.
4. Let cool and mix in dried cranberries.

Wild Rice and Mushroom Frittata

Ingredients:

- 6 eggs
- 1/4 cup milk
- 1/2 cup cooked wild rice
- 1/2 cup mushrooms, sliced
- 1/4 cup shredded cheddar cheese
- 1 tbsp butter
- Salt and pepper to taste

Instructions:

1. Sauté mushrooms in butter until soft.
2. In a bowl, whisk eggs, milk, salt, and pepper. Stir in wild rice and mushrooms.
3. Pour into a greased oven-safe skillet, sprinkle with cheese.
4. Bake at 375°F (190°C) for 15-20 minutes until set.

Chokecherry Syrup Pancakes

Ingredients:

Pancakes:

- 1 cup all-purpose flour
- 1 tbsp sugar
- 1 tsp baking powder
- 1/2 tsp baking soda
- 1/4 tsp salt
- 1 cup buttermilk
- 1 egg
- 1 tbsp melted butter

Chokecherry Syrup:

- 2 cups chokecherries
- 1 cup water
- 1 cup sugar

Instructions:

1. For syrup, simmer chokecherries and water for 15 minutes. Strain and return liquid to pot.
2. Add sugar and simmer until thickened.
3. For pancakes, mix dry ingredients. Whisk wet ingredients separately and combine.
4. Cook pancakes on a hot griddle until golden.
5. Serve with chokecherry syrup.

Cornmeal Johnny Cakes with Maple Butter

Ingredients:

Johnny Cakes:

- 1 cup cornmeal
- 1 cup boiling water
- 1/2 cup milk
- 1 tbsp butter, melted
- 1/2 tsp salt
- 1/2 tsp baking powder

Maple Butter:

- 1/2 cup butter, softened
- 2 tbsp pure maple syrup

Instructions:

1. In a bowl, mix cornmeal and boiling water. Let sit for 5 minutes.
2. Stir in milk, melted butter, salt, and baking powder.
3. Heat a skillet over medium heat and grease lightly. Drop batter by spoonfuls and cook for 2-3 minutes per side.
4. For maple butter, whisk butter and maple syrup together until smooth.
5. Serve Johnny Cakes warm with maple butter.

Rye Toast with Homemade Berry Jam

Ingredients:

Jam:

- 2 cups mixed berries (blueberries, raspberries, strawberries)
- 1/2 cup sugar
- 1 tbsp lemon juice

Toast:

- 4 slices rye bread, toasted
- Butter for spreading

Instructions:

1. In a saucepan, combine berries, sugar, and lemon juice. Simmer for 10-15 minutes, mashing berries slightly. Let cool.
2. Spread butter on rye toast and top with homemade jam.

Maple Pecan Sticky Buns

Ingredients:

Dough:

- 2 1/2 cups all-purpose flour
- 2 tbsp sugar
- 1 tsp salt
- 2 1/4 tsp active dry yeast
- 3/4 cup warm milk
- 3 tbsp butter, melted
- 1 egg

Filling:

- 1/2 cup brown sugar
- 1 tsp cinnamon
- 1/4 cup butter, softened

Topping:

- 1/2 cup pecans, chopped
- 1/4 cup butter, melted
- 1/4 cup maple syrup

Instructions:

1. Mix warm milk, yeast, and sugar. Let sit for 5 minutes. Add flour, salt, butter, and egg, knead into a dough. Let rise for 1 hour.
2. Roll out dough into a rectangle. Spread softened butter and sprinkle cinnamon sugar. Roll up and slice into buns.
3. In a baking dish, mix melted butter, maple syrup, and pecans. Place buns on top. Let rise for 30 minutes.
4. Bake at 350°F (175°C) for 25 minutes. Flip out of the pan to reveal sticky pecan topping.

Bison Sausage and Egg Breakfast Sandwich

Ingredients:

- 2 bison sausages
- 2 eggs
- 2 English muffins, toasted
- 2 slices cheddar cheese
- 1 tbsp butter

Instructions:

1. Cook bison sausages in a skillet over medium heat until browned.
2. Melt butter in the same skillet and fry eggs.
3. Assemble sandwiches by placing a sausage, egg, and cheese on each toasted English muffin.

Apple Butter Toast with Canadian Cheddar

Ingredients:

- 4 slices sourdough or rye bread
- 1/2 cup apple butter
- 4 slices Canadian cheddar

Instructions:

1. Toast bread until golden brown.
2. Spread apple butter on each slice.
3. Top with a slice of cheddar and serve.

Classic Poutine Breakfast Bowl

Ingredients:

- 2 russet potatoes, diced
- 2 tbsp butter
- 1/2 cup cheese curds
- 1/2 cup breakfast gravy (or classic poutine gravy)
- 2 fried eggs
- Salt and pepper to taste

Instructions:

1. Heat butter in a skillet and fry diced potatoes until golden brown.
2. Top with cheese curds and pour hot gravy over.
3. Place a fried egg on top and serve warm.

Maple Glazed Donuts

Ingredients:

Doughnuts:

- 2 cups all-purpose flour
- 1/4 cup sugar
- 1 tbsp baking powder
- 1/2 tsp salt
- 1/2 cup milk
- 1 egg
- 3 tbsp butter, melted
- Oil for frying

Glaze:

- 1/2 cup pure maple syrup
- 1 cup powdered sugar
- 1 tbsp milk

Instructions:

1. Mix flour, sugar, baking powder, and salt in a bowl.
2. In another bowl, whisk milk, egg, butter, and mix with dry ingredients.
3. Roll out dough and cut into doughnut shapes.
4. Heat oil to 350°F (175°C) and fry doughnuts until golden brown.
5. For glaze, whisk maple syrup, powdered sugar, and milk. Dip warm donuts in glaze and let set.

Grilled Arctic Char and Poached Egg Toast

Ingredients:

- 2 slices sourdough bread, toasted
- 4 oz grilled Arctic char
- 2 poached eggs
- 1 tbsp chopped chives

Instructions:

1. Grill Arctic char until flaky and cooked through.
2. Poach eggs in simmering water for 3-4 minutes.
3. Place grilled fish on toasted bread, top with a poached egg, and garnish with chives.

Cranberry Walnut Breakfast Bread

Ingredients:

- 2 cups whole wheat flour
- 1/2 cup rolled oats
- 1/4 cup honey
- 1 tsp baking soda
- 1/2 tsp salt
- 1/2 cup dried cranberries
- 1/2 cup chopped walnuts
- 1 cup buttermilk

Instructions:

1. Preheat oven to 350°F (175°C).
2. Mix flour, oats, baking soda, salt, cranberries, and walnuts in a bowl.
3. Stir in honey and buttermilk to form a dough.
4. Transfer to a greased loaf pan and bake for 40-45 minutes.

Maple Walnut Granola Bars

Ingredients:

- 2 cups rolled oats
- 1/2 cup chopped walnuts
- 1/4 cup dried cranberries
- 1/2 cup pure maple syrup
- 1/4 cup almond butter
- 1/2 tsp cinnamon

Instructions:

1. Preheat oven to 325°F (165°C).
2. Mix oats, walnuts, cranberries, and cinnamon in a bowl.
3. Heat maple syrup and almond butter in a saucepan until combined. Pour over oat mixture and stir.
4. Press into a lined baking dish and bake for 20-25 minutes. Let cool before cutting into bars.

Smoked Trout and Dill Scramble

Ingredients:

- 4 eggs
- 1/4 cup milk
- 2 oz smoked trout, flaked
- 1 tbsp fresh dill, chopped
- 1 tbsp butter
- Salt and pepper to taste

Instructions:

1. Whisk eggs, milk, salt, and pepper in a bowl.
2. Heat butter in a skillet and pour in eggs, stirring gently.
3. Add flaked trout and dill, cooking until eggs are just set.
4. Serve warm with toast.

French Canadian Crêpes

Ingredients:

- 1 cup all-purpose flour
- 1 1/4 cups milk
- 2 eggs
- 1 tbsp melted butter
- 1 tbsp sugar
- 1/2 tsp salt
- 1/2 tsp vanilla extract

Instructions:

1. In a bowl, whisk together flour, milk, eggs, butter, sugar, salt, and vanilla until smooth. Let rest for 10 minutes.
2. Heat a non-stick skillet over medium heat and grease lightly.
3. Pour a small amount of batter into the pan, swirling to coat the bottom.
4. Cook for 1-2 minutes, then flip and cook for another 30 seconds.
5. Serve warm with maple syrup, fresh fruit, or powdered sugar.

Bacon and Egg Bannock Sandwich

Ingredients:

- 2 pieces of bannock
- 4 slices bacon
- 2 eggs
- 2 slices cheddar cheese
- 1 tbsp butter
- Salt and pepper to taste

Instructions:

1. Cook bacon in a skillet until crispy. Remove and set aside.
2. In the same pan, melt butter and fry eggs to desired doneness. Season with salt and pepper.
3. Slice bannock in half, layer with cheddar cheese, bacon, and egg. Serve warm.

Maple Baked Beans on Toast

Ingredients:

- 2 cups cooked navy beans
- 1/2 cup pure maple syrup
- 1/2 cup diced onion
- 1 tbsp Dijon mustard
- 1/4 cup ketchup
- 1/2 tsp salt
- 4 slices toasted rye bread

Instructions:

1. In a saucepan, mix beans, maple syrup, onion, mustard, ketchup, and salt. Simmer for 15 minutes.
2. Spoon baked beans over toasted rye bread. Serve warm.

Roasted Pumpkin and Spice Muffins

Ingredients:

- 1 cup pumpkin purée
- 1 1/2 cups all-purpose flour
- 1/2 cup brown sugar
- 1 tsp baking powder
- 1/2 tsp baking soda
- 1 tsp cinnamon
- 1/2 tsp nutmeg
- 1/2 tsp salt
- 2 eggs
- 1/4 cup melted butter
- 1/2 cup milk

Instructions:

1. Preheat oven to 375°F (190°C).
2. In a bowl, mix flour, sugar, baking powder, baking soda, cinnamon, nutmeg, and salt.
3. In another bowl, whisk pumpkin, eggs, butter, and milk. Combine with dry ingredients.
4. Spoon batter into muffin tin and bake for 18-20 minutes.

Wild Berry Yogurt Parfait

Ingredients:

- 1 cup mixed wild berries (Saskatoon berries, raspberries, blueberries)
- 1 cup Greek yogurt
- 1/4 cup granola
- 1 tbsp honey

Instructions:

1. Layer yogurt, berries, and granola in a glass.
2. Drizzle with honey before serving.

Cheddar and Apple Omelet

Ingredients:

- 3 eggs
- 1/4 cup milk
- 1/2 cup shredded cheddar cheese
- 1/2 apple, thinly sliced
- 1 tbsp butter
- Salt and pepper to taste

Instructions:

1. Whisk eggs, milk, salt, and pepper in a bowl.
2. Melt butter in a skillet over medium heat. Pour in eggs.
3. Once eggs begin to set, add apple slices and cheddar.
4. Fold omelet and cook for another minute. Serve warm.

Saskatoon Berry Breakfast Crisp

Ingredients:

Filling:

- 2 cups Saskatoon berries
- 1/4 cup sugar
- 1 tbsp cornstarch
- 1/2 tsp cinnamon

Topping:

- 1/2 cup rolled oats
- 1/4 cup flour
- 1/4 cup brown sugar
- 1/2 tsp cinnamon
- 1/4 cup butter, melted

Instructions:

1. Preheat oven to 375°F (190°C).
2. Toss berries with sugar, cornstarch, and cinnamon, then place in a baking dish.
3. Mix oats, flour, brown sugar, cinnamon, and melted butter. Sprinkle over berries.
4. Bake for 25-30 minutes until golden. Serve warm.

Sweet Corn Fritters with Honey Butter

Ingredients:

Fritters:

- 1 cup corn kernels
- 1/2 cup all-purpose flour
- 1/4 cup cornmeal
- 1/2 tsp baking powder
- 1/4 tsp salt
- 1 egg
- 1/4 cup milk
- 1 tbsp butter

Honey Butter:

- 2 tbsp butter, softened
- 1 tbsp honey

Instructions:

1. In a bowl, mix flour, cornmeal, baking powder, salt, egg, and milk. Fold in corn.
2. Heat butter in a skillet and drop spoonfuls of batter. Cook for 2 minutes per side until golden.
3. Mix honey and butter together. Serve fritters warm with honey butter.

Maple Cinnamon Overnight Oats

Ingredients:

- 1/2 cup rolled oats
- 1/2 cup milk
- 1 tbsp pure maple syrup
- 1/2 tsp cinnamon
- 1/2 cup diced apples or berries

Instructions:

1. In a jar, mix oats, milk, maple syrup, and cinnamon.
2. Stir in fruit and refrigerate overnight.
3. Stir before serving.

Classic Western Sandwich

Ingredients:

- 3 eggs
- 1/4 cup diced ham
- 1/4 cup diced bell pepper
- 1/4 cup diced onion
- 1 tbsp butter
- 2 slices bread, toasted

Instructions:

1. In a bowl, whisk eggs and season with salt and pepper.
2. Sauté ham, bell pepper, and onion in butter. Add eggs and scramble.
3. Place egg mixture between toasted bread slices. Serve warm.

Butter Tart Waffles

Ingredients:

Waffles:

- 2 cups all-purpose flour
- 1 tbsp sugar
- 1 tbsp baking powder
- 1/2 tsp salt
- 1 1/2 cups milk
- 2 eggs
- 1/4 cup melted butter

Butter Tart Topping:

- 1/2 cup brown sugar
- 1/4 cup butter
- 1/4 cup heavy cream
- 1/4 cup chopped pecans or raisins

Instructions:

1. Preheat waffle iron and grease lightly.
2. In a bowl, mix flour, sugar, baking powder, and salt.
3. Whisk milk, eggs, and butter separately, then combine with dry ingredients.
4. Cook waffles according to waffle iron instructions.
5. For topping, melt butter and brown sugar in a saucepan. Stir in cream and pecans/raisins.
6. Pour over warm waffles before serving.

Roasted Hazelnut and Maple Porridge

Ingredients:

- 1 cup rolled oats
- 2 cups milk or water
- 1/4 cup roasted hazelnuts, chopped
- 2 tbsp pure maple syrup
- 1/2 tsp cinnamon
- 1/2 tsp vanilla extract

Instructions:

1. In a saucepan, bring milk to a simmer. Add oats and cook for 5 minutes, stirring occasionally.
2. Stir in maple syrup, cinnamon, and vanilla extract.
3. Top with roasted hazelnuts and serve warm.

Cranberry and Sunflower Seed Energy Bites

Ingredients:

- 1 cup rolled oats
- 1/2 cup dried cranberries
- 1/4 cup sunflower seeds
- 1/4 cup honey
- 1/4 cup almond or peanut butter
- 1/2 tsp cinnamon

Instructions:

1. In a bowl, mix oats, cranberries, sunflower seeds, cinnamon, honey, and nut butter.
2. Roll into small balls and refrigerate for 30 minutes before serving.

Canadian Bacon Breakfast Pizza

Ingredients:

- 1 store-bought or homemade pizza crust
- 1/2 cup pizza sauce
- 1/2 cup shredded mozzarella cheese
- 4 slices Canadian bacon, chopped
- 2 eggs
- 1 tbsp chopped chives
- 1/2 tsp black pepper

Instructions:

1. Preheat oven to 425°F (220°C).
2. Spread pizza sauce over crust, top with cheese and Canadian bacon.
3. Crack eggs on top and season with black pepper.
4. Bake for 12-15 minutes until eggs are set.
5. Sprinkle with chives and serve.

Caramelized Apple Pancakes

Ingredients:

Pancakes:

- 1 1/2 cups all-purpose flour
- 1 tbsp sugar
- 1 tsp baking powder
- 1/2 tsp salt
- 1 1/4 cups milk
- 1 egg
- 2 tbsp melted butter

Caramelized Apples:

- 1 apple, sliced
- 2 tbsp butter
- 2 tbsp brown sugar
- 1/2 tsp cinnamon

Instructions:

1. In a bowl, whisk together flour, sugar, baking powder, and salt.
2. In another bowl, mix milk, egg, and melted butter. Combine with dry ingredients.
3. Cook pancakes on a greased skillet over medium heat.
4. For apples, melt butter in a pan and sauté apple slices with brown sugar and cinnamon for 5 minutes.
5. Serve pancakes topped with caramelized apples.

Peameal Bacon Eggs Benedict

Ingredients:

- 4 slices peameal bacon
- 2 English muffins, halved and toasted
- 4 eggs
- 1 tbsp white vinegar
- 1/2 cup hollandaise sauce

Instructions:

1. In a skillet, cook peameal bacon over medium heat until golden brown.
2. Bring a pot of water to a gentle simmer, add vinegar, and poach eggs for 3-4 minutes.
3. Place peameal bacon on toasted muffins, top with poached eggs, and drizzle with hollandaise sauce.

Maple Chia Seed Pudding

Ingredients:

- 1/4 cup chia seeds
- 1 cup milk (or almond milk)
- 2 tbsp pure maple syrup
- 1/2 tsp vanilla extract

Instructions:

1. In a jar, mix chia seeds, milk, maple syrup, and vanilla extract.
2. Stir well and refrigerate overnight.
3. Serve chilled, topped with fruit or nuts.

Homemade Rhubarb Jam on Toast

Ingredients:

Jam:

- 2 cups chopped rhubarb
- 3/4 cup sugar
- 1 tbsp lemon juice

Toast:

- 4 slices rye or sourdough bread, toasted

Instructions:

1. In a saucepan, cook rhubarb, sugar, and lemon juice over low heat for 15 minutes, stirring often.
2. Spread warm or cooled jam over toast.

www.ingramcontent.com/pod-product-compliance
Lightning Source LLC
LaVergne TN
LVHW081332060526
838201LV00055B/2605